LARISSA ANDRUSYSHYN

Proof

■

LIVRES
DC
BOOKS

Cover art by Sonia Roy, colagene.com.
Author photograph by James Bouthillier.
Book designed and typeset by Primeau Barey, Montreal.
Edited by Jason Camlot.

Legal Deposit, Bibliothèque et Archives nationales du Québec
and Library and Archives Canada, 4th trimester, 2014.

Library and Archives Canada Cataloguing in Publication
Andrusyshyn, Larissa, 1978- , author
Proof/Larissa Andrusyshyn.
Poems.
ISBN 978-1-927599-31-0 (bound).
ISBN 978-1-927599-30-3 (pbk.)
I. Title.
PS8601.N456P76 2014 C811'.6 C2014-907000-4

For our publishing activities, DC Books gratefully acknowledges the financial support of the Canada Council for the Arts, of SODEC, and of the Government of Canada through Canadian Heritage and the Canada Book Fund.

Canada Council for the Arts Conseil des Arts du Canada

Société de développement des entreprises culturelles Québec

Printed and bound in Canada.
Interior pages printed on FSC® certified environmentally responsible paper.
Distributed by Fitzhenry and Whiteside.

FSC www.fsc.org MIX Paper from responsible sources FSC® C095263

DC Books
PO Box 666, Station Saint-Laurent
Montreal, Quebec H4L 4V9
www.dcbooks.ca

Contents

I

Assume There Exists x

Assume There Exists x

The distance between x and y is equal to 1 day and 2 hours[1] ∴ I've updated my relationship status accordingly ∴ Notebooks contain your notes on Dostoyevsky's existentialist angst ∴ When it rains, I wonder what time it is in Vancouver ∴ Your copy of *The Invisible Man* remains on the shelf in my room ∴ The shirt with the pearl buttons has lost your smell ∴ I have driven the nail of "time heals all wounds" deep into the floor planks of my memory ∴ I have troubled sleep ∴ Your name brandishes archives ∴ I can't stand the sight of lichen or bridges ∴ Oranges taste like sawdust ∴ I drink but I don't drunk dial ∴ I make the bed now ∴ I made the bed ∴ The bed is made.

■

1 4,899.5 km; allowing for an average speed of 80 km/hour on the Trans Canada HWY

Axis

X is a calculator
made of springs and polymers.
He is arithmetic with a display screen.

His partner is *Y*, with a tag and zipper
Y declares the abstract space.

X holds an axis, a grilled cheese sandwich and
  regular calls home.
Y holds that we are made of exploded stars.

Y feels bad for all the other *Y*'s
in alternate universes:
For the *Y* whose arm was bitten off by a coyote,
the *Y* who sells commercial real estate in Wichita,
the *Y* who stitches labels on shoes in
  a Cambodian sweatshop.

X doesn't think of other dimensions,
the universes where he is the shepherd
and she spins the wool.

X draws unproven things:
two headed unicorns, an octopus with wings,
love-strung astrophysicists,
and portraits of writers with drinking problems.
He never draws *Y*–
the imaginary unit.

Y adopts a new syntax for him–
learns the names of northern constellations,

Cassiopeia, Draco, Orion,
as he plots the charts.

When he moves away,
he leaves pin holes in the map for her to find.

■

Euler's Identity

Kiss me over string theory,
use the word *elegant.* Let's fall in love
in the absence of it.

Write anecdotes on circle relations,
diameter to circumference. The numbers scatter
    like enemies
behind the lines. The decimal is upstairs, recovering.

$e^{i\pi} + 1 = 0$

Give me expressions of the most beautiful theorem
    ever written.

Irrational, imaginary,
numbers to map the universe.
You hand me your phone number on a crack-head
    street corner.

The equality has made it all ordered for us.

It's proven and like love
we know it has its truth,
but I have no idea what it means.

■

Fermat's Last Theorem

Hanc marginis exiguitas non caperet.

On the edge, the tragedy is what spills over,
the note scribbled there beside the text–
a problem described as *beautiful,*
but without proof.

"Math is not tragic," you said.

I think of the notes you didn't leave,
which may have sufficed
to convince me of an infinite.
I need a symbol to outlast death and departure–
to know the value of one action
is fixed.

Fermat's *marvelous* discovery–
too large for the margin to contain.

The noose around the mathematician's neck
is what he knows but cannot demonstrate–
some driven to suicide over the betrayal
of their own hypotheses.

Leaving the blackboard and its elliptic curves,
checking back again and again:
it was still there.
A twentieth century proof.
For the obsessed, what will take its place?

We'd remain conjecture,
unsolved, with a sort of window, a way in.

It was not relief, but despair that met him there.
After hundreds of years and several collaborations
a solution is like a bullet; the stumbling stops.

The problem is so small he could cover it with his thumb.

■

Ǝ!n

The envelope on which you drew an elephant
reminded me of the mark of a river
on a map of the Saguenay.
I haven't been back.

The envelope, there exists only one,
a memory where you hand me your jacket in the street.
I trip over my feet,
the snowfall drops a veil, absorbs the sound.

In storms like tonight
a memory edges from my brain
for the path to the beach,
the drumfire.

■

Valence

Love ionic,
Love chemical.
Love that claims you with valances.
Our brains pump oxytocin,
and then, love ionic.

We lived as ice, dense, crystalline–
the polar hydrogen bond
on a couch playing XBOX on split screen.

Then dilution crept in.

Water is external, alien. I cannot drown.
We are solid,
and were always this.

I bit into an oyster,
dying muscle, the taste of sea grass,
and salt: oxidation.

Paint peels from bedroom walls,
electrons drift beyond orbit, things change,
the frost melts.

We are altered, we come apart.
The last time I saw you–the indifferent window
a thousand miles away,
your reflection turned back.

I become a wound packed with safety glass,
precipitation, sealed in a climate shift.

I have loosened, untied, become solvent.

■

Variables

In high school our hair frizzed in gym class,
we saved quarters for jukeboxes and skipped
lunch to play pool.

We practised addition on bathroom walls,
boys' initials became the variables.
We showed our work
and wrote commutative quantities–
we always arrived at two.

l+n

The plus sign there like a promise,
an elevator caught between floors.

Myself and being
plus the one boy,
an irrational number

An equation is a relationship after all.

■

Equivalent

Turing's cyanide laced apple
and the sharp decline of peaches.

We were killers.
We died often.

He is the skin, the husk,
whereas sleep is the flight.

Guilt, the focused lens:
a cold spring, the scant harvest.

We are content to gnaw the pit.

■

Math

I think I have found its defining feature
beauty in method,
a long thread of do-gooders
plugging in numbers.

Formulas aren't important anymore.
It is not uncommon to hear physicists
represent the ratio of the physical
to the evolutionary conundrum.

Almost every other branch
is seen three-dimensionally,
inspired by the theories
for those unlucky few who haven't yet discovered
aversion to numbers,

because life is easy for mathematicians.

■

1

I am composed of two parts,
the me and the absence.

The glyph and its outline.
I am not the mysterious chasm
from which your hand returns full.

I am the container, the buried coffin.

In a slew of birds–maybe gray ones,
each has a ribcage locking its gears
around one perfect furious heart.

Hear me in the click of bolt and pin.

Unary, the first impair,
the empty product.

I sought two, binary, monad,
a chain of operations.
I wanted to leave the integer in favor of the equation.
Naught adjacent, the single entity
with the heavy digit. I put the *one* in *lonely.*

A truant, I live between nothing and the Rom-Com cliché
and I want to add you.

■

In Which Planck's Constant Informs the Brokenhearted

I hear about a breakup so bad the guy hires a plane
to tow a banner with the physics equation for
  Planck's constant.

In the city of Denver where he lives
the chess players on 16th Street will look up,
maybe she will too.

The spray painted stencil flowers, the poems inked
onto subway walls, we're the same, graffiti artists and poets
seeking the eye of some passing pedestrian.

For him there is comfort in the numbers
that express the fabric of light as he poses for
  minimum wage
in the University art department.
If a photon can be measured, a value can be assigned
  to anything.

He totes his backpack across campus, loves the weight of it
which is a constant.
In quantum theory this is expressed by *h*.

Even to the muscle fibers that strain to be still and hold,
until its time for another pose.
This reminds him of the delicate structure of the universe.
The difference between particle and wave.

Every breakup is a mess of equations,
of abstract and precise numbers, divisions
and remainders. You need to hire a plane, a chessboard
and a can of paint to make them balance again.

■

Collide

He mentions how Dostoyevsky wrote stories
to pay off gambling debts. And we play poker.

We met because cells divide. To break
is the first thing we do.

We became
marks made to retrace the distance back
to when dinosaurs walked the Earth.

Before, we were nothing
and our parents, nothing.

The particles broke from particles, collided and the sound
they made was creation–
phonics of accidental combinations.

Look back.

Before his hands and the pocket aces,
the absence of hands.

Genealogical amputations.

Before spleen, splenectomy.
before absence, him.

■

Missed Connection W4M

Male, wearing black tuque at La Belle Province on
St. Laurent Blvd.

Last Thursday night, your beard peppered with
poutine sauce.

Me: wearing a black dress, waterproof boots.

You: handsome, dejected.

You had your hockey stick with you. Left curve, composite,

tape torn loose hanging like a noose above your head.

Tell me you know the word to describe the feel of the puck
leaving that curve on a perfectly timed wrist shot, my
life depends on it?

■

II
Memory Circus

Malaparte's Frozen Horses

In his memory they are running from fire
with the odor of the dead.

Horses placed in the ruin of war,
in this case, a bombardment in the siege of Leningrad.
From the stables of the soviet artillery
they flee a wildfire.
A stall is an enclosure and also a pause.

They break free in a panic, hundreds of bodies
burst from the forest and into lake Ladoga.
In an instant the water received them
and was changed.
Water became ice and froze them in place.

In his journal Malaparte describes
a sheet of horse heads still and cool as marble,
all facing the shore.

Death is suspended, not like a carousel,
but a landscape of slaughter that remains. *Hold your horses*
he whispers.

How the flesh gave in, their passage halted midstride.
The charred skin smells of pine and wood smoke.
By morning their teeth are still bared.

The Trinket Room

Museum of Broken Relationships, Zagreb

Brown dog of blown glass,
two poems tacked to the wall,
a flowerless cactus,
a pair of black boots left by the door.
A jewelry box, a belt buckle,
and a wind up puppy that plays the symbols.

I am preparing my catalogue
I have curated a collection–

A copy of *The Blank Slate* with an unbroken spine.

A Rubik's cube, unsolved.

Three sketchbooks with unfinished paragraphs.

A drawing of two whales in blue dry-erase marker.

I am the custodian of the bookends
that I keep in the middle of the shelf
nose to nose.

And the note scrawled on a page-a-day calendar
Don't wait up for me.

Migration

An earthquake in Chile shook us so bad
it changed the Earth's axis.
The path of migration deviated
in tiny degrees. Days became shorter.

The arctic is a runway of snow
and Polar bears take a route
passed down, in blood, in skin–
reading the land, the magnetic field
that drives the body to sea.

The hunt is seasonal.
The bears move with weather changes.
They follow the food, the source,
to breeding grounds off the coast of Churchill.

Your name spoken in sleep, muscle memory,
the surprise of what the brain digs up.
Grief is more like an orbit, something you can't help
but come back to.

I received your messages, the photographs
taken at drag queen bingo halls,
where the women slip in and out
of character.
I can't remember how I got home.

If This Were a Love Poem

I'd question its existence. It would stink
of dopamine and stimulants, cocaine saccharine
and the fabric of a happy girl's red dress.

I'd doubt it was necessary or useful; a junk mail flyer,
carefully wedged into the seat
of the #63 bus on Girouard.

I'd find it unfamiliar, a solar flare or a rat with wings.
I'd jar it in formaldehyde, wrong place, wrong time,
maybe the world ends. Whenever.

I'd put it in hiding. Lower the price for quick sale.
Tear the bar code off and mail it to the Prime Minister
with a note that says: *it was always you.*

Arbutus

The flowers appear
while the previous year's fruit ripens.
After pollination Arbutus pauses,
It's a shrub that delays its fruit, keeps calm.

I feign to pronounce it correctly,
ask you to point it out when I visit.

I will not change emergency contacts, delete
messages, photographs. I don't touch the books
or dust the shelves.

This is the respite before the fruit.
Later we can resume jokes about naming babies
    after produce.

I'll give up in the sound that pings off the mountains.
The sound that pings because you are quiet.

I stay in your bed while you go to class. You think
I'm monotonous, I am exhausted
from being so far away, from the fear
of you loving me less and less.

I'll keep it to myself,

I'll give it up. Love your back, your eyes
as you explain the function of plant life dormancy
in this temperate climate.

Dovima With the Elephants

Cirque D'Hiver, Paris. 1955

One escapes the frame, three-toed rebel.
The others lift an obedient right foot.
The model is an unconventional beauty.

Skin and silk,
rule of threes, her arm arches upward,
their trunks follow.

Throwing their heads back,
to grip some long memory of the river Mara;
for the mud, the give of earth underfoot.

Here, the elephants are in surrender,
the chains are visible.

I'm obsessed, lovesick over these great beauties–
Elephant man, elephant in the room, the circus side show
pulled from the roaming herd. The skinny girl
in the fashion spread pulled from the streets of
  New York City–
En Vogue and the world over is captive.

Pachyderm and curio
my brothers, my brothers,
pacing beneath Napoleon's circus tent–
let loose your three ringed trumpet call.

Elvis in the Madame's House

Like a childhood cat, I have become
something you had once loved.

The thrift-store find is all rhinestones and Liberace glitter.
This is my third act.

Beneath my coat I wear a layer of stranger's fingerprints
in soft-focus wax.

Look for me next to the crowds who take photographs
of their heads in the mouth of Siegfried's tiger.

This Tussaud's house has bent me permanently,
posed me like a servant, kneeling on the ever-lit stage
with a soundtrack that plays an endless loop of thankyous.

Somewhere there is a place like Topelo,
where the mantles are lined with collectors plates,
and clocks that shimmy and sing,
with my face, every hour, on the hour.

My hometown has no memory
of a life before me.

But here I've been poured, shaped
and kept safe during the business hours–

Escapologist

You let the ropes loose, a Houdini
freeing himself.
Where I am the chain. Pure delay.

Harry eludes every bind and bolt.
When the mechanism won't give,
there's Bess with a kiss
and the key in her mouth.

Behind the curtain he slips the chains off
emerges like the rabbit from a black hole top hat.
White rabbit.
Black hat.

Hung in a straightjacket from a crane in New York City,
his face as calm as a milkman's.

I am not the clasp coming loose.
I am the traffic below.

For the Coney Island sideshow man,
death is a latch that can't be picked.

I thought I was drowning in the box beside you,
but I was the water, the hinge, the lock.

Topsy the Elephant

Coney Island, 1903

I invoke you. To return
to darken my door
like a patient in the wards, to wander sick
calling out the crime.

Repetition is the schizophrenic's crutch.

Edison appears in your dreams as a rat
holding two electrodes in his teeth.

Smuggled, long-lashed and train-wrecked
you are indentured, obey
even as a man throws a lit cigar in your mouth
from the crowd.

Now how many elephants can swallow fire?
Or, be the torch the inventor ignites his career on?

The inconvenient elephant, sold
from under the billowing big top
to spill the mystery of electricity like a confession.

If you told the story they'd call you mad–
death row began like a circus side show.
The electric chair pictured by every mumbling murderer.
Topple a giant with an alternating current.

Your last meal: carrots laced with potassium cyanide.
The audience knows nothing of life or limb, the loveless
trainers and the silence you took with you.
They drag the wires over.
The light bulb flickers. Your breath
you keep.

The Magician's Assistant

In sequins, I belong in the wooden box.
I lay and never speak.
I smile and he leads me in.

In the pine of the pine
I smell his aftershave.
This is how I like him best,
I'm on the inside with my secrets.

When the saw digs its teeth
the sound is my disassembly.
He rolls the box halves,
pulls me apart.

I am best in pieces, the crowd hushed,
he resurrects me when he brings them back.

For his next trick
he hangs me up,
spins the wheel
and gathers a handful of knives.

The Dove

It's the way we spot yetis and whales,
subtle movement draws the eye steady as a hook.
You stumble upon it like wreckage;
the dove on your bookshelf is a deviation.

He snuck in, you say
I didn't know how to ask him to leave.

He is perched on Rushdie.
You are calm, as if birds always rise from libraries
to roost on wires and pictures of skylines–
all those filaments intersecting,
fictions and feathers the color of nacre.

I can't help thinking of the magician somewhere
reaching into his black hat,
the vanished pitiful apparatus.

No trick of eye or mirror,
I cover the bird with a towel and step outside
to the beckoning skies of Brooklyn.

Canary Space Program

With the suspension
of the space program
birds remain the last
explorers in the sky.

Physics equations scrawled
in chicken scratch
on the inside of deposed shuttles
describe the path.

Canaries with clipped wings
are cancelled flight missions,
singing, caged, in beige kitchens.

Passenger Pigeon

The last passenger pigeon is archived
in a block of ice. I can't decide

what to keep.
Your breath in sleep when I'm awake,

a fleeting passerby, you
in a doorway, the skipped beat.

My memory of you as a bird,
who belongs to wind and treetop.

A man formed in a swarm of them–
my love was instant.

How we grow extinct, annihilated
before we even know we're hunted.

Flocks a mile wide once obscured the sky
before they were brought to ground.

Marriage beds were made with dowries
for pillows stuffed with passenger down.

Remains we burn or bury–
purge the ash and bone.

Lovers doze on plucked gestures,
you smell of horizons, grow restless in this warm kitchen.

III
Parts and Holes

As is With the Butcher

Be clean and sanitary.
Sharpen the blade and cut across the grief.
Halve and quarter, the carcass is a quotient.

Cuts of meat–this necessity to divide,
wherein body equals despair, attachment–
connective tissue.

Seam between the muscle
with a knife. Write an elegy
for the bone.

Substitute marrow for her,
the unoccupied hook.

Such workmanship,
the color, light pink to cherry red.
exudative of stress,
at this one low level–a fine pacing
in the flaws.

Primal cuts, forequarter–
shank, chuck, plate and rib.
Feel for some marbling,
the hand recoils.

On the Sale of a Duplex

Nothing will remember the old apartment,
it was a reservoir with zero as a placeholder.

I'm too old for a quick death. I'll have this
slow decline. I'd rather write elegies than odes
I'm more comfortable with agony, prefer the pin prick
to the kiss.

The contractor's truck parked out front
and a slowly filling dumpster.

This is whiskey Sunday, walking by our old place
where we played poker and drank American beer.
Through the front door I see it's gutted, bones bare.

I'm a coward, nothing's changed,
It's a form of art; clinging to the scraps.

But I'd rather see it burn than gyprocked into
some sweetheart's new condo.

Self Portrait

I'm tired of the book shelves,
the stacks I never get to.
The typewriter, with the dry ribbon
I didn't replace.

I get my bearings in detritus.
There was no catastrophe,
just slow erosion.

When I've unwound it all, stretched the skin
of my life out, it'll shrink back to a small strip,
dry out and blow like dust.

I keep looking back, twenty, ten, two,
years ago.

If given the choice,
what if I were there?

Back at the shore
of a previous me, drifting close.

Propriety of Nouns

A clutch of eggs, a batch of bread,
flight of pigeons, conspiracy of ravens.

A clout of cats, dozing,
Sunday morning carillon of bells,
old town cobble stone with its curse of painters
and promise of barmen.

An amble of walkers,
of cruise ship buffalo,
a tangent of tourists,
crush of shoppers
and prey of nuns.

Beyond the walled city,
smell of saltwater,
the glean of herring, the draught of fish.

The stony beach with its clutter of spiders, of starlings,
clew of worms,
and cowardice of curs,
a fling of sandpipers
a charm of finches.

A blush of boys,
a giggle of girls.

A rabble of gnats
and a flotilla of ships,
a mess of lives cast off.

Dandelion

The spore that gathers
like a girl, lifted that sometimes kicks
into the wind.

When the world stops for once,
she prepares a flood
in which to lose herself.

Supernova

We are made of star stuff
–Carl Sagan

The iron in your blood
once burned at the core
of a distant star.

You and I are three explosions–
calcium, carbon, magnesium,
expelled at the speed of light.

We are built
and we separate
in turbulence.

We are elemental–
peering through telescopes
at all that we don't know–
Plasma held together by its own gravity, a star
is creation and death.

Granny sweaters and haircuts replace
the old you. Pixilated remnants
of a changing world.

One burst and the foundations
of planets and bodies and sand are laid.

bones and blood–
what we call
            living things.
And dust, does it remind you of me?

IIII

Entomologist's Index

The Entomologist's Index

After Justin Schmidt

1.0
Sweat bee: light, ephemeral,
The hymenoptera venom slips in your skin;
a nuisance that lingers in tones of vanilla and bergamot:
flare on your tongue from a cup of hot tea:
the snub of an acquaintance in the street.

1.8
Acacia ant: rare and biting,
don't be fooled by the tiny beltian body
this is a smoky single malt wound:
stiffing the waitress, a blip of static shock.

2.0
Honey Bee: sting benchmark;
a pin in the thorax places a specimen against velvet:
the sting is a hammer mistakenly driven onto thumb,
    tinfoil in your teeth.
A form rejection letter from a prominent journal.

3.0
Paper wasp: a cluster of hangovers:
the pain is dislocated; writhing.
Enzymes fire with the pace of traitors–
cramp and shudder; the bite of a layoff
or the grating drag of an income tax audit.

Woodlouse

Armadillidium

Genus of many names, slip
easy as a squeeze beneath a damp stone.

Potato bug, boat-builder, pill bug–
holds aliases like segments of a jointed exoskeleton,
in defense they fold into a perfect ball
rolled in the palms of curious children.

Leg-breathing identity thief,
a crustacean, conqueror of gardens
and habitats far from the sea.

I dug you up under the old floorboards
you scattered under my father's voice
calling me home.

Dung Beetle

In the desert your compass is cast skyward
for a night that pulls its collar tight.

Scientists place cardboard hats on beetles
to cover the dorsal eyes, obscure the Milky Way.

Stars are points on the chart, light fixtures,
like crumbs dropped on the path.

Polaris for dead reckoning,
but with nothing to draw a dotted line from–
wouldn't you know they trample each other,
go in circles, disoriented like drunks?

When life hands you lemons
remember you hatched in dung.

Underrated shit-kicker.
Sheath-winged stargazer.

You make a world of it, a brooding ball,
like Atlas, the sky is a map on your shoulders.

Rolling across the desert,
manning the observatory.

Scarab

Painted on the walls of pyramids
chasing the sun out of darkness.

Myth of beetle dragging the ball of light,
the world appears
they chant *I become,*
I become.

Milk and honey, Coleopteran,
they carve up your back
with the names of kings
envy your firm heart.

Sacred amulet piece, grounded
by your story and every sunrise
is proof.

They scatter you in tombs.

Accessory

We immunize against boredom,
accessorize with rhinestones
and dollar store glitter.

When everything's been done before,
is there anything sadder
than bedazzled cockroaches?

Swarovski crystal
glued on the carapace.

Majesty sputters, as ghost-fingers
flutter on satin blouses.
Affix a leash to the beast, tether it to a pin.

Every fashion forward girl
wears a medal for bravery as the creature
scurries against her heart.

The wingless captive,
is a writhing beauty.

The Sorrows of the Ladybird Beetle

For Shannon

Her pain is shown
against the head of a match
for scale.

She vanishes in cold seasons: diapause.

Named in the middle ages,
when farmers prayed against pests.
Her red carapace followed the scourge.

Red of the virgin's cloak,
equal spots for joy and sorrow.

Beetles account for the majority of the biomass on Earth–
which accounts for her and husks shed in molting seasons.

Her color deters,
associates with a bad taste–
bitter crunch of apples.

Stranger among the aphids and hemiptera;
She is not a true bug with mouthparts that pierce.

Clade of beetle, that one ancestor.

She has a segmented heart,
and bleeds in self-defence, by reflex,
without puncture.

Bed Bug

Insemination is hypodermic–
the term: traumatic.

She is a magnet of warmth,
he enters to a still rising resistance.

It's the male's lot to be given a sword
and the quickest route to a female's heart.

The call of carbon dioxide brings them;
breath is blood.

In the colony drawn by exhalations,
hers is a cavity as good as scripture,
hers is a tradition to brace for impact.

On the Consumption of Several Floor Joists; East Nashville

The dettrivore in on a salvage mission,
this is no infestation in the bread box, no Brooklyn
    dwelling pest,
the taxonomy lumps them with the cockroaches;
white ant of the order blattodea-
the termite is a keen recycler.

It's symbiosis; the work of unlikely codependents,
in this case a microbe that lives in the guts of termites.

Named for the moving flagella,
a tuft of synchronised tentacles
that call to mind images Lovecraft's monsters,
a Cthulhu resembling a winged cephalopod,
performs intestinal alchemy;
turning wood into sugar. Cellulose into glucose.

Soluble, digestible, a floor board is a carbohydrate.

The termite is obligate
he makes way in the world with silent partners.

Digestive hermit,
buried in the business, chews through fiber
delivers the gold.

The Diving Bell Spider

You would expect despair,
a glacier-fed, submerged heartbreak.
A girl tossed overboard–
drops anchor.

With nothing familiar, look how she
spins a life underwater.
It's not alchemy, but a silk bell–
her breath, a chamber.

She brings home only death and sex–
asphyxiates her prey.
Skilled as a glassblower,
she sighs nostalgic into a bubble
and fixes it in place.

There is a trace of the surface,
a reflection on her abdomen
that jitters with water's movement.
Recognition is voluntary.

Cast off in exile, home becomes
eupnea, mooring, anywhere
the oxygen can be replenished.

She could drown,
loose with her airs.

Give her
the wind.

Elegy of Wingless Bugs

Praise movement, belly contractions
and the temporarily grounded,

the crawl space where you amount to something.
I was a memory once, once I was real.

On the fire escape where I first learned
that I was dated and you were moving

I named bugs that don't fly–
grub, maggot, cockroach.

The ones left footless and limbless
by kids who hold the wings and pull.

We're left so damaged we can't even writhe.

Footless and limbless. You could be loved
but they fall out of that.

I was left, collapsed,
it was necessary to presume everyone dead.

There is a fault line in my oxygenated blood
that pushes everything off course.

So I built a casket fit for two.

Hieroglyphica

No one suspects the scaly winged pick pocket.

A mouth like a straw unfolds
to drink up the tears of sleeping birds.

The moth is turning a wound inside out,
release in the orchid and tree bark.
Stomach contents: grief and disaster.

In the dark forests of Madagascar
a transient in imago;
this Lepidoptera hunts the lacrimal.

Imagine the dry eyes of sparrows,
the slender-billed flufftail, the cuckoo,
all waking with a sadness they can't shake.

The Mating Posture of Diplopoda

Bi-lateral–

They are born legless.

First moult occurs in detritus,
She is built in segments
that curl like sinistral gastropod shells.

Millipedes can fuck in body armour.
Hinge and dry heat.

A narrow passage for a nest
in which to applaud the leaves
that made the bed.

Entwine anatomically
and you can breed.

But always have a plan B–
when there's a thousand legs
to lose your lover.

Practise DIY genetics, parthenogenesis.
Channel the agave apomixes that clone themselves
along the Karoo.

She can trigger the egg cell
like trip wire.

Venom

Perhaps this is the natural
outcome of interactions
–Justin Schmidt

You left
the barbed quill, our era
you said.

Thud of an empty glass.

This is not a simple brush
with the poison leaf.
The stinging insect is all about intimacy.

You see how we must be close enough
to strike, break in.

This is hands-on, love,
mandibles are syringes.

keep the old shirts,
cracked knuckles, your new appointments.
Throwaway nickels, leftovers
you say.

Toxins interfere, a rash, a scent–
venom is injected with purpose.

No long distance sniping, crosshairs
and scope, crouched on the rooftop
has the nervous trigger finger.

You'll need to be close–
hands, body and mouth;
skin on skin.

Ecdysis

The sawfly sheds its skin.
Attachment is for the parasite.

You pale, soft bodied shedder.
A skin cell, a city with a girl inside.

Why carry a world on your back
when your shell can be re-grown.

Whereas I become the constant
in an equation about gravity,

you left and came back again.
Grief came later.

I thought of you, up the coast, waiting
for your mother's drive to chemotherapy.

The homes on the road to Chicoutimi–
dioramas of lives fused by obligation.

Exoskeleton, fully grown now,
ants die in the skin they're born in.

Encumbrance is learned. I inhabit my husk,
drag the shell like a June beetle with its carapace.

Gnat

A ghost of them at dusk,
drawn to the lachrymal, the eye.
However contemptible
the dipterid is bold

Even the smallest gnat
is as much the subject
in the bowl of cherry pits,
the cup of coffee, spoiled
by the slick hairless body, afloat.

How are they made,
these small considerations?

Which of us
in the natural of natural
can ignore the buzzing,

O lord of forests and the stagnant waters
of our eyes
how can we?

Sex Lives of Leopard Slugs

Drawn by a scent,
a body without bone–
move with the ease of silk.

Upward, slugs seek
an overhang.

Hermaphrodite contortionists
spin on a rope of mucous.
Entwined, dangling aerialists in courtship.

The intrusive mind, endless swing
as if overtaken by a current.
Optical tentacles, skirt and mouth,
fringe against foot, press
in a knot that spins.

The penis is in the slug's head:
they both evert a phallus and tangle.
It can take hours
to unwind the appendages.
They drop like a seed
to its place on the earth.

Earworm

In a cluttered room you call me by the wrong name.
You are most endangered, a dainty bone in the jaw of
a yellow bird. I had wanted to catch your eye. It's open mic
night and the comedians are talking over each other. The
man with his hand in my hair whispers "you're as cold as
the tundra." I take whiskey and write my name on all the
coasters like a chorus I can sing to myself over and over.

Proof

Is in the pudding,
or activate the yeast let the dough proof

of purchase, receipt.

A galley, facsimile for job verification.

A measure of strength, content,
the bourbon's bite is equivalent
to 7⁄4 times the alcohol by volume.

Evidence delivered in a trial,
a photograph or sworn declaration.

Proofread, edit, check for mistakes.

The quality of armour,
        see: resistance, fire-proof, gunpowder testing.

The observable truth,
or the series of steps taken
to a resolution.

A convincing solution for a formula that declares the x
    is an unknown,
the equations you scrawl to find your ex.

The instrument with which the surgeon probes
the depth of wounds.

■

Q.E.D.

quod erat demonstrandum

Notes on Symbols

■ Denotes the end of a proof in place of the traditional phrase Q.E.D., an abbreviation for *quod erat demonstrandum,* "which had to be demonstrated" in Latin.

∴ Used in proofs before logical consequences; meaning therefore; such that or hence.

∃!n A uniqueness quantification meaning there exists exactly one of.

Acknowledgements

Some poems from this collection have appeared in *Carte Blanche, CV2* and *Encore Literary Magazine* and I am grateful to the editors of those publications.

"Euler's Identity" (2012) and "The Diving Bell Spider" (2014) were shortlisted for Arc Magazine's Poem of the Year.

"Elvis in the Madame's House" was shortlisted for the Malahat Review's Open Season Award for Poetry (2014).

Thanks to DC and to Jason Camlot, I am blessed to work with him, a talented and attentive editor.

I am humbled by the wonderful Wired Writing Studio at the Banff Centre and the artists I met there. I am indebted to the many friends I made and wrote with, drank with or performed with and especially: Jennifer, Katherine, Erika, Buffy, Phil, Janet and Brea who were exceptional buddies. Also, many thanks to the music of Wichita Elk and the heiresses to ping pong dynasties.

And Jennifer Still, my brilliant mentor. You should be so lucky to know someone with such careful hands and warmth. Her feedback helped shape this manuscript and I cherish the time I got to work with her.

Sources

This is a work of poetry. Names, sciences and incidents are products of the author's imagination. Any resemblance to math or the study of entomology, real or imagined, is purely coincidental.

I am indebted to the following for providing the research or inspiration that launched this book:

Justin O. Schmidt's "Connoisseur's Sting Index" (borrowed with permission) and the documents he generously provided including his paper on venom evolution and entomology.

The final stanza of "Euler's Identity" is borrowed from Benjamin Pierce's reflections on Euler.

Quantum Physics for Poets (Prometheus Books, 2011) by Leon M. Lederman and Christopher T. Hill.

The podcasts *Radiolab* and *This American Life* remain my constant fodder.

Wikipedia. Because.

Larissa Andrusyshyn's first book *Mammoth* (DC Books 2010) was shortlisted for the QWF First Book Prize and the Kobzar Literary Award. Her poems have been shortlisted for *Arc Magazine*'s Poem of the Year and the *Malahat Review*'s Open Season Award. She works with a local non-profit to offer creative writing workshops to at-risk youth. She lives, writes and is planning her zombie apocalypse survival strategy in Montreal.

Proof